Pebble® Plus

Exploring the Galaxy
Neptune

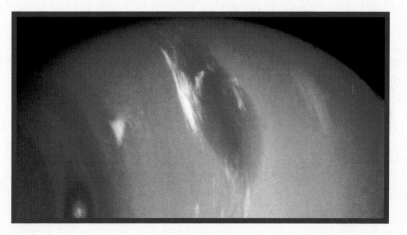

by Thomas K. Adamson

Consulting Editor: Gail Saunders-Smith, PhD

Consultant: James Gerard
Aerospace Education Specialist, NASA
Kennedy Space Center, Florida

Capstone press®

Mankato, Minnesota

Pebble Plus is published by Capstone Press,
151 Good Counsel Drive, P.O. Box 669, Mankato, Minnesota 56002.
www.capstonepress.com

1 2 3 4 5 6 12 11 10 09 08 07

Library of Congress Cataloging-in-Publication Data
Adamson, Thomas K., 1970–
    Neptune / by Thomas K. Adamson.—Rev. and updated.
    p. cm.—(Pebble plus. Exploring the galaxy)
    Includes bibliographical references and index.
    ISBN-13: 978-1-4296-0732-2 (hardcover)
    ISBN-10: 1-4296-0732-7 (hardcover)
    1. Neptune (Planet)—Juvenile literature. I. Title. II. Series.
QB691.A33 2008
523.48'1—dc22
                                                            2007004454

Summary: Simple text and photographs describe the planet Neptune.

Editorial Credits
Mari C. Schuh, editor; Kia Adams, designer; Alta Schaffer, photo researcher

Photo Credits
Digital Vision, 5 (Venus)
NASA, 1, 7, 15, 17, 21; JPL, 5 (Jupiter); JPL/Caltech, 5 (Uranus), 13
PhotoDisc Inc., cover, 4 (Neptune), 5 (Mars, Mercury, Earth, Sun, Saturn), 11 (both); Stock Trek, 9, 19

Note to Parents and Teachers

The Exploring the Galaxy set supports national science standards related to earth science. This book
describes and illustrates the planet Neptune. The photographs support early readers in understanding the text.
The repetition of words and phrases helps early readers learn new words. This book also introduces early
readers to subject-specific vocabulary words, which are defined in the Glossary section. Early readers may
need assistance to read some words and to use the Table of Contents, Glossary, Read More, Internet Sites,
and Index sections of the book.

Table of Contents

A Blue Planet

Neptune is the eighth
planet from the Sun.
Neptune looks bright blue.

Neptune

The Solar System

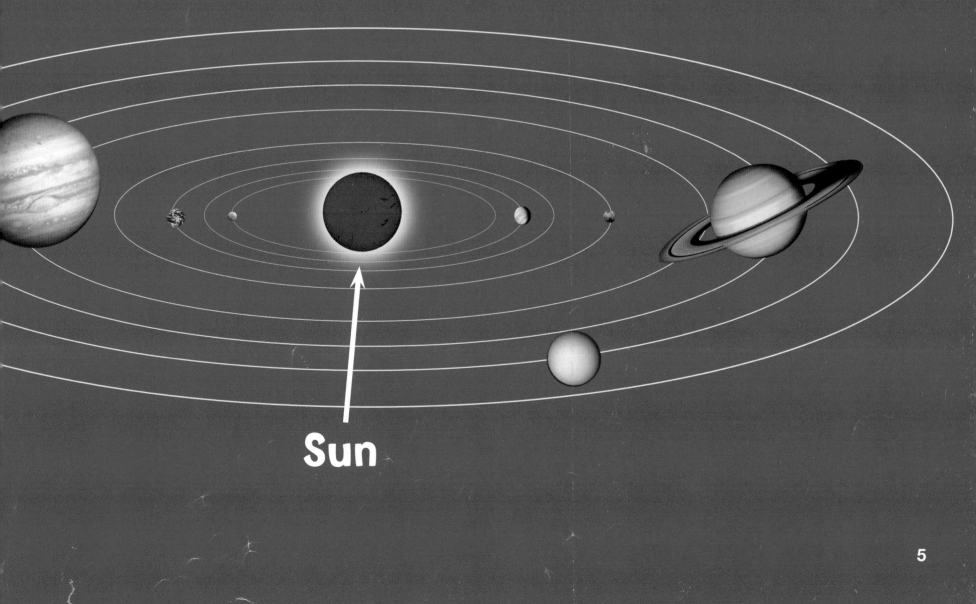

Sun

Neptune is a big ball
of gases and clouds.
It is called a gas giant.

White clouds move

across Neptune.

The clouds often

change shape.

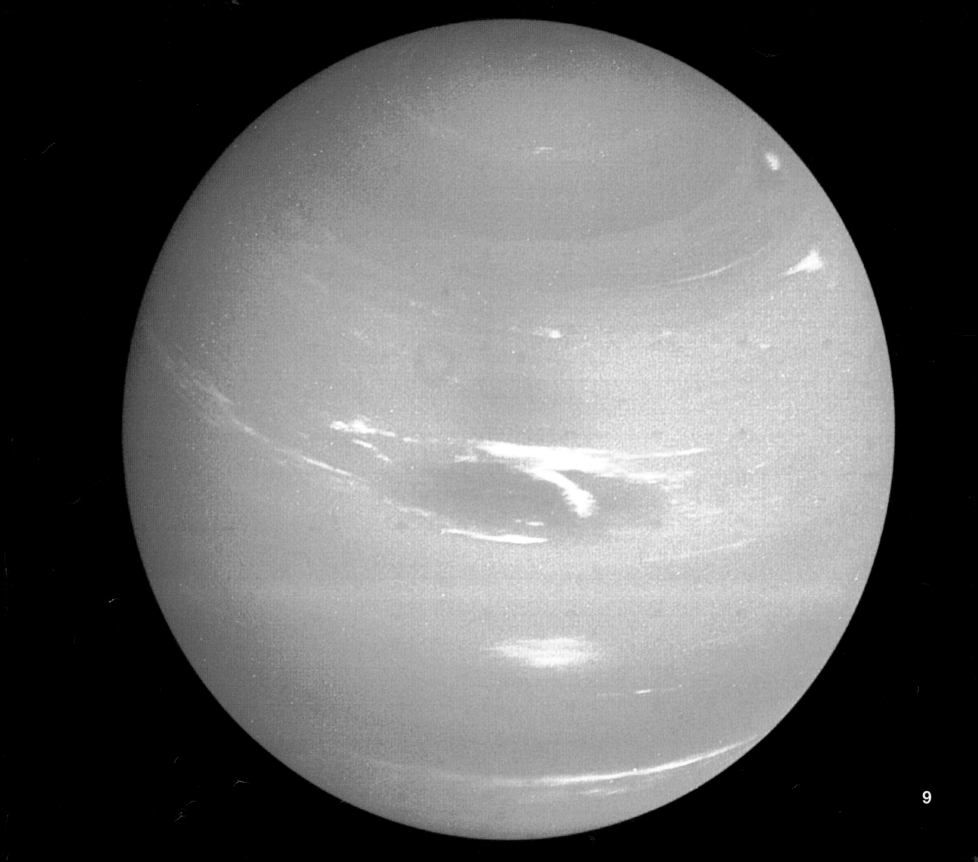

9

Neptune's Size

Neptune is the fourth
largest planet.
Neptune is almost four times
wider than Earth.

Neptune

Earth

Neptune's Moons

At least 11 moons

move around Neptune.

Most of the moons

are small, icy chunks of rock.

13

Neptune's largest moon

is called Triton.

It is made of rock and ice.

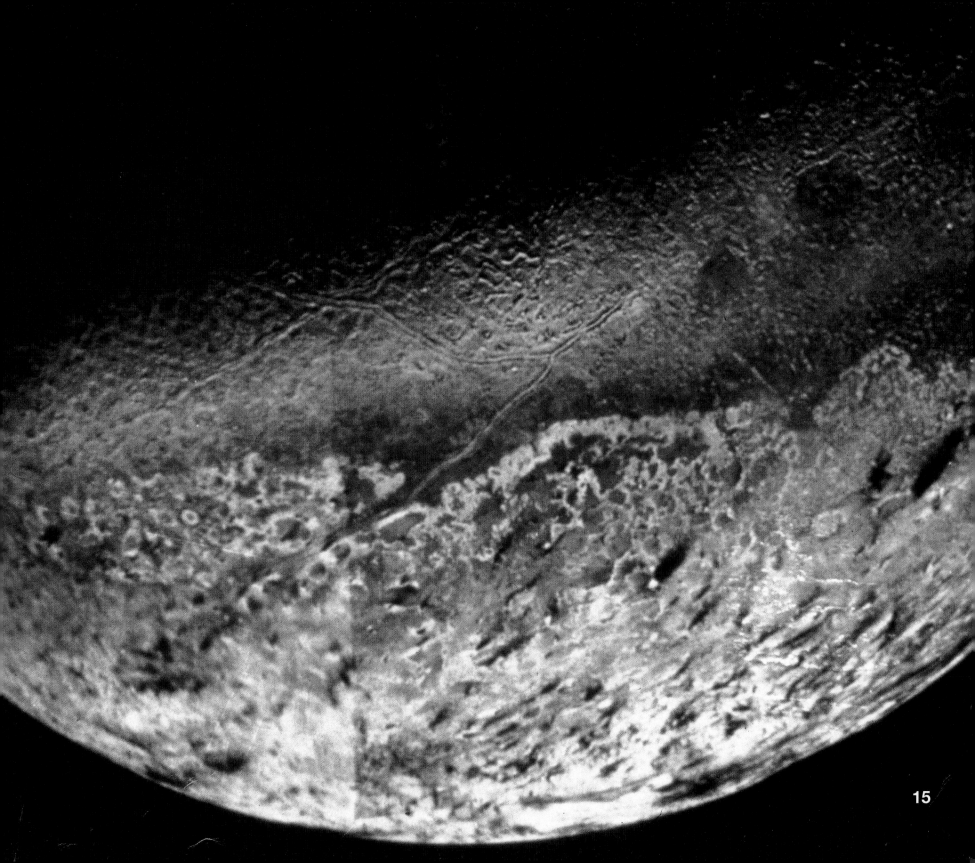

Triton probably looks
like the dwarf planet Pluto.
Triton is one
of the coldest places
in the solar system.

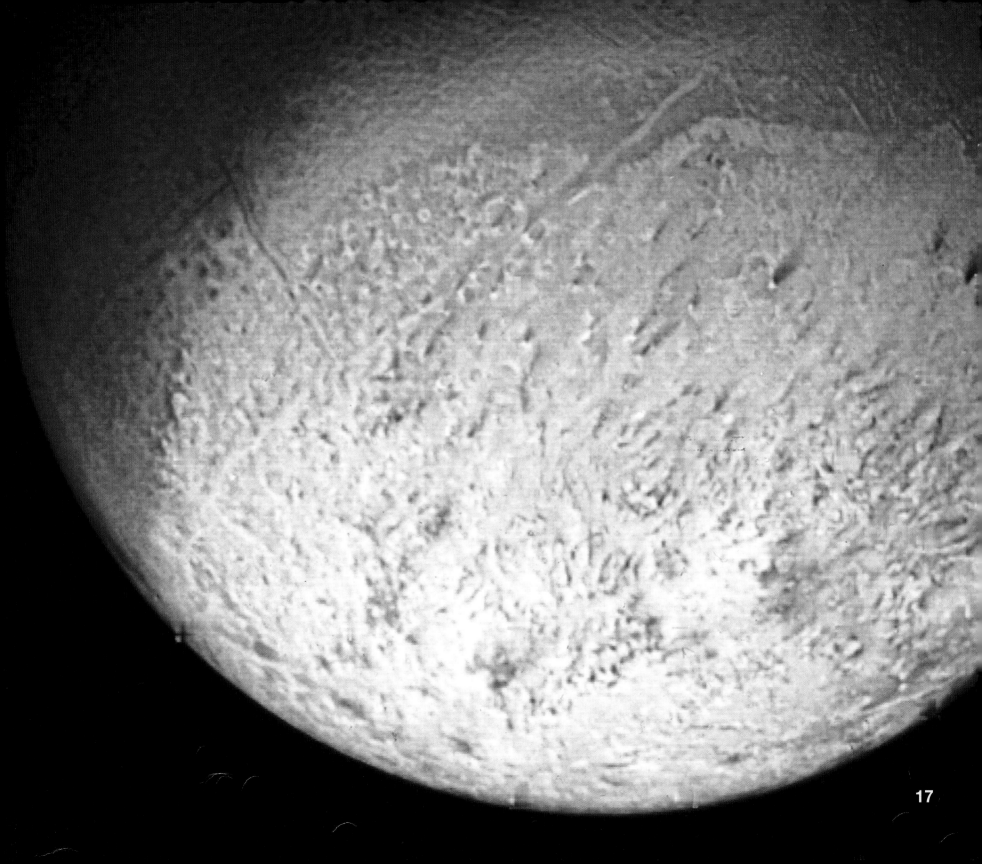

People and Neptune

Neptune does not have

a solid surface.

People could not live

on Neptune.

People cannot see Neptune
without a telescope.
Neptune is too far away.

Glossary

dwarf planet—a round object that moves around the Sun, but is too small to be a planet

gas—a substance, such as air, that spreads to fill any space that holds it; Neptune is called a gas giant; the other gas giants are Jupiter, Saturn, and Uranus.

moon—an object that moves around a planet

planet—a large object that moves around the Sun; Neptune is the eighth planet from the Sun; there are eight planets in the solar system.

Sun—the star that the planets move around; the Sun provides light and heat for the planets.

telescope—a tool people use to look at planets and other objects in space; telescopes make planets and other objects look closer than they really are.

Read More

Olien, Rebecca. *Exploring the Planets in Our Solar System.* Objects in the Sky. New York: PowerKids Press, 2007.

Wimmer, Teresa. *Neptune.* My First Look at Planets. Mankato, Minn.: Creative Education, 2007.

Winrich, Ralph. *Neptune.* First Facts: The Solar System. Mankato, Minn.: Capstone Press, 2008.

Internet Sites

FactHound offers a safe, fun way to find Internet sites related to this book. All of the sites on FactHound have been researched by our staff.

Here's how:

1. Visit *www.facthound.com*

2. Choose your grade level.

3. Type in this book ID **1429607327** for age-appropriate sites. You may also browse subjects by clicking on letters, or by clicking on pictures and words.

4. Click on the **Fetch It** button.

FactHound will fetch the best sites for you!

Index

Word Count: 125
Grade: 1
Early-Intervention Level: 14

24